A Mother's
L O V E

Fiorenzo Di Lorenzo (c.1440-1522/5) *Virgin and Child*

Grange
BOOKS

Sandro Botticelli (1444/5-1510) *Madonna of the Magnificat*

A Mother's
L O V E

Compiled By Anna Nicholas

Philippe Mercier (1689-1760) *Burckhardt Tschudi with his Wife and Two Children*

A selection of poems and quotations

Acknowledgments

The Publishers would like to acknowledge the following
for permission to reproduce copyright material:
Page 8, Faber & Faber for 'My Youngest Daughter
Getting up in the Morning' by Adèle Davide (from
Messages compiled by Naomi Lewis); Page 9, Faber &
Faber for 'Distracted the Mother Said to Her Boy' by
Gregory Harrison (from *Messages* compiled by Naomi
Lewis); Page 10, Bloodaxe Books Limited for
'Elementary (for Rufus)' by Linda France (from *New
Women Poets*); Page 11, Faber & Faber for 'Partly
Because' by Ursula Laird (from *Messages* compiled by
Naomi Lewis); Page 12, Bloodaxe Books Limited for
'Jonathan' by Janet Fisher (from *New Women Poets*);
Page 14, Faber & Faber for 'Ballad of the Dreamy Girl'
by Edith Roseveare (from *Messages* compiled by Naomi
Lewis); Page 16, Bloodaxe Books Limited for 'Kicking
against the Walls' by Katrina Porteous (from *New
Women Poets*); Page 17, David Highams Associates for
'First Foetal Movements of My Daughter' by Penelope
Shuttle (from *The Orchard Upstairs*); Pages 25 and 39,
Jonathan Cape and The Hogarth Press for 'Pietà' and 'A
Carol' by C. Day Lewis, (from *The Poems of C. Day
Lewis*); Pages 31, 32 and 34, Faber & Faber for 'To My
Mother', 'Full Circle' and 'Oh, Yes, My Dear' from *The
Collected Poems of Walter de la Mare*; Page 36
Heinemann Educational Books for 'Plaits' by Tabitha
Tuckett, first published in *Young Writers, 24th Year.*

The Publisher has made every effort to trace copyrights
holders of material reproduced within this compilation.
If, however, they have inadvertently made any error
they would be grateful for notification.

Many thanks to Paperchase, London for kindly allowing
us to use their papers.

Pictures courtesy of Bridgeman Art Library

Published in 1994 by Grange Books
An imprint of Grange Books PLC
The Grange, Grange Yard
London SE1 3AG

ISBN 1 85627 616 3

Printed in Italy

Adolf Eberle (1843-1914) *The Happy Family*

When I was only five years old,
    My mother, who was soon to die,
Raised me with fingers soft and cold,
        On high;

Until, against the parlour wall,
    I reached a golden paper flower.
How proud was I, and ah! how tall,
            That hour!

'This shining tulip shall be yours,
    Your own, your very own,' she said;
The mark that made it mine endures
        In red.

I scarce could see it from the floor;
    I craned to touch the scarlet sign;
No gift so precious had before
        Been mine.

A paper tulip on a wall!
    A boon that ownership defied!
Yet this was dearer far than all
        Beside.

Real toys, real flowers that lavish love
    Had strewn before me, all and each
Grew pale beside this gift above
            My reach.

Ah! now that time has worked its will,
    And fooled my heart, and dazed my eyes,
Delusive tulips prove me still
        Unwise.

Still, still the eluding flower that glows
    Above the hands that yearn and clasp
Seems brighter than the genuine rose
        I grasp.

So has it been since I was born;
    So will it be until I die;
Stars, the best flowers of all, adorn
        The sky.

Edmund Gosse

Mary Cassatt (1844-1926) *Mother and Child*

She is like snow
fallen from the roof
when she rises;
the windows in the room below
rattle

My Youngest Daughter Getting Up in the Morning Adèle Davide

F. Smallfield (1829-1915) *The Apple Room*

Distracted the mother said to her boy
'Do you try to upset and perplex and annoy?
Now, give me four reasons – and don't play the fool –
Why you shouldn't get up and get ready for school.'
Her son replied slowly, 'Well, mother, you see,
I can't stand the teachers and they detest me;
And there isn't a boy or a girl in the place
That I like or, in turn, that delights in my face.'

'And I'll give you two reasons,' she said, 'Why you ought
Get yourself off to school before you get caught;
Because, first, you are forty and, next, you young fool,
It's your job to be there. You're the head of the school.'

Gregory Harrison

I ask my son what he knows of earth,
of properties of metal,
the rings in the heart of wood,
what shapes he can trace in the air,
how deep is the blue of water;
remind him to take care of fire.

He has a dangerous fondness for fire,
my son, learning the lessons of earth;
knows magnets are science, metal,
observes their attraction through water.
He's aware that a kite, and he, needs air,
the paper he'd miss so much is wood.

We scramble hand in hand through the wood
near our house, feeling the damp earth
spring under our feet, the lapping of water
in the silence. The cold air
makes him cough so we go home to the fire,
welcomed by kettle's singing metal.

His toys are plastic; mine were metal,
with sharp corners. They rusted in water.
Now the fashion's back for wood,
carved and painted trains, trucks and fire engines.
Things have changed. This earth
I thought I knew, and love, is mutable as air.

My son was four the year the air
blew from the east, poisoned by fire,
a fire kindled with no wood.
The smell of my sweat was metal.
We couldn't trust rain, milk or earth,
were afraid to drink the water.

He loves to play in water,
and I to watch him, in the tenuous air
of summers. I lean against knotted wood,
by the river glinting metal.
As certain as flames in fire
we're held in the breath of earth.

I pray to the gods of air, goddesses of wood
and water, that he'll be saved from fire,
and save, like precious metal, all he knows of earth.

Linda France b.1958

Bernard Fleetwood Walker (b.1892) *The Family*

10

Partly because of the mistakes I made
I felt obliged to say to my son
be kind to people
be a kind seller of seeds
or petrol pump attendant instead of an unkind lawyer
or an uncaring director of personnel.

I could only say it once
and he has gone away
chasing butterflies
but what he does to them
if they are caught
if they are in his power
I am never there to see.

Ursula Laird

Mary Cassatt (1844-1926) *Mother and Child*

11

French homework due in Tuesday scribbled

in red on the back of the hand not holding

the roller-ball slim-line, black ink, he

confidently analyses *Macbeth* with his

favoured stylistic flourishes and gothic

Js. Bulbous tips of fingers, half moon

nails bitten to the quick, scrape raw

nostrils. Grown six inches in a year,

hair like wire, witty with teachers

when he meets them in the supermarket,

he knows how far he can go, they tell us.

Janet Fisher b.1943

Paul Albert Besnard (1849-1934) *The Artist's Family*

13

A pigtail dangled down my back,
I was just sixteen years.
One day my mother came and flicked
a duster round my ears.

'Don't sit there writing poetry,
go dust your room instead!
With all this nonsense you won't earn
the butter on your bread!'

She often scolded me, but I
stepped lightly as a bird
and went on dreaming through the day
as if I had not heard.

What could I say?
My mother would never understand.
So I wrote only secretly,
the duster in my hand.

When finally I learned to cook,
I often heard her tell:
'To keep your future husband sweet,
you'll have to feed him well!'

'And how do men keep women sweet?'
She gave me no reply
but went on cooking, and I saw
her shake her head and sigh.

Edith Roseveare

Carl Larsson (1855-1919) *Mother and Child*

Charles Angrand (1854-1926)
Portrait of the Artist's Mother Sewing

15

It's starting to break my sleep.

A rich and alien germ

Riddles my body, deep

Inside, inseparable,

Wanting rid of me, kicking

The walls, striking the land

That holds and feeds it. Tell me -

A woman would understand -

What is the worm that quickens

Out of my mould and climbs

Onward to leave me dying,

A traveller in time?

I sing to it in confinement.

Rage, my baby; grow

Strong with the secret, darling -

The dead won't let you go.

Katrina Porteous B.1960

Mary Cassatt (1844-1926) *Mother Bathing her Child*

16

Berthe Morisot (1841-1895) *The Cradle*

Shadow of a fish
The water-echo
Inner florist dancing
Her fathomless ease
Her gauzy thumbs
Leapfrogger, her olympics in the womb's stadium

First Foetal Movements of My Daughter Penelope Shuttle b.1947

17

Thomas Brooks (1818-1891) *Sweet Dreams*

Edith Rockefeller McCormick, daughter of John D. Rockefeller 1872-1932

Edith McCormick always maintained a large staff in her huge and magnificent house. One rule applied to them all, from the first butler to the personal maid's assistant: they were not permitted to speak to her. Only once was that rule broken. One evening, in 1901, when Edith McCormick's young son was suffering fron scarlet fever, a dinner party was in progress at the family's country retreat in Lake Forest. During the meal the news arrived that the unfortunate boy had died. Following a discussion in the servant's quarters, the tragic news was whispered to Mrs. McCormick. Mrs. McCormick merely nodded her head, and the dinner party continued without pause.

Upon my lap my sovereign sits
And sucks upon my breast;
Meantime his love maintains my life
And gives my sense her rest.
    Sing lullaby, my little boy,
    Sing lullaby, mine only joy!

When thou hast taken thy repast,
Repose, my babe, on me;
So may thy mother and thy nurse
Thy cradle also be.
    Sing lullaby, my little boy,
    Sing lullaby, mine only joy!

I grieve that duty doth not work
All that my wishing would;
Because I would not be to thee
But in the best I should.
    Sing lullaby, my little boy,
    Sing lullaby, mine only joy!

Yet as I am, and as I may,
I must and will be thine,
Though all too little for thyself
Vouchsafing to be mine.
    Sing lullaby, my little boy,
    Sing lullaby, mine only joy!

Richard Rowlands 1565-1630?

20

Mary Cassatt (1844-1926) *Bathing*

Sweet dreams, form a shade
O'er my lovely infant's head,
Sweet dreams of pleasant streams
By happy silent moony beams.

Sweet sleep, with soft down
Weave thy brows an infant crown.
Sweet sleep, Angel mild,
Hover o'er my happy child.

Sweet smiles, in the night
Hover over my delight;
Sweet smiles, Mother's smiles,
All the livelong night beguiles.

Sweet moans, dovelike sighs,
Chase not slumber from thy eyes.
Sweet moans, sweeter smiles,
All the dovelike moans beguiles.

Sleep, sleep, happy child.
All creation slept and smil'd
Sleep, sleep, happy sleep,
While o'er thee thy mother weep.

Sweet babe, in thy face
Holy image I can trace.
Sweet babe, once like thee
Thy maker lay and wept for me,

Wept for me, for thee, for all,
When he was an infant small.
Thou his image ever see,
Heavenly face that smiles on thee,

Smiles on thee, on me, on all,
Who became an infant small.
Infant smiles are his own smiles;
Heaven and earth to peace beguiles.

William Blake (1757-1827)

21

A child's a plaything for an hour;
    Its pretty tricks we try
For that or for a longer space –
    Then tire, and lay it by.

But I knew one that to itself
    All seasons could control;
That would have mock'd the sense of pain
    Out of a grievèd soul.

Thou straggler into loving arms,
    Young climber-up of knees,
When I forget thy thousand ways
    Then life and all shall cease.

Mary Lamb 1765-1847

E. Zampighi (1859-1944) *Tantalizing*

John Callcot Horsley (1817-1903) *The New Dress*

Actor Clifton Webb was devoted to his mother, who had campaigned on his behalf with producers and directors throughout his career. A tireless exhibitionist, she was still dancing the can-can at Hollywood parties in her 90th year. When she finally died, Webb's health rapidly declined. 'Poor dear,' remarked Coward. 'The late sixties is rather late to be orphaned.'

Frans Hals (1580-1666) *Family Group in a Landscape*

Sandro Botticelli (1444/5-1510) Pietà

Naked, he sags across her cumbered knees,
Heavy and beautiful like the child she once
Aroused from sleep, to fall asleep on the next breath.

The passion is done,
But death has not yet stiffened him against her,
Nor chilled the stripling grace into a dogma.
For a timeless hour, imagined out of marble,
He comes back to his mother, he is all
And only hers.

And it is she whom death has magnified
To bear the burden of his flesh — the arms
Excruciated no more, the gash wiped clean.
A divine, dazed compassion calms her features.
She holds all earth's dead sons upon her lap.

Pietà C. Day Lewis 1925-1972

Two women living alone in the same house had babies within three days of each other. One baby died, and its mother stole the other while the mother slept, substituting the corpse of her own baby. Although the other woman noticed the deception, the first woman refused to relinquish the baby. So they came before King Solomon, each claiming that the living child was hers. The king commanded his officers to bring the sword and when it was brought ordered that the baby be cut in two; one half would be given to one woman and the other half to the other. The rightful mother, stirred with love and pity for her child said, 'O my lord, give her the living child, and in no wise slay it.' But the other woman said , 'Let it be neither mine or thine, but divide it.' The King, perceiving that the compassion of the first woman had identified her as the true mother, ordered that the baby be given to her.

Augustus John (1878-1961) *A Family Group*

26

You must
wake and call
me early, call
me early,
mother dear

Alfred Lord Tennyson (1809-1892)

Lester Sutcliffe (fl.1880– c.1930) *Mother and Child Beneath the Blossom*

When Jesus therefore saw his mother, and the disciple standing by, whom he loved, he saith unto his mother, Woman behold thy son! Then saith he to the disciple, Behold thy son! And from that hour the disciple took her into his own home.

John 19:26-27

Pieter de Hooch (1629-c.1684) *Family Portrait on a Terrace*

Sir George Hayter (1792-1871) *Portrait of a Mother and Her Four Daughters*

John Singer Sargent (1856-1925) *Mrs Carl Meyer, later Lady Meyer; and her Two Children*

Thine is my all, how little when 'tis told
    Beside thy gold!
Thine the first peace, and mine the livelong strife;
Thine the clear dawn, and mine the night of life;
    Thine the unstained belief,
    Darkened in grief.

Scarce even a flower but thine its beauty and name,
    Dimmed, yet the same;
Never in twilight comes the moon to me,
Stealing through those far woods, but tells of thee,
    Falls, dear, on my wild heart,
    And takes thy part.

Thou art the child, and I — how steeped in age!
    A blotted page
From that clear, little book life's taken away:
How could I read it, dear, so dark the day?
    Be it all memory
    Twixt thee and me!

To My Mother Walter de la Mare 1873-1956

When thou art as little as I am, Mother,
And I as old as thou,
I'll feed thee on wild-bee honeycomb,
And milk from my cow.
I'll make thee a swan's-down bed, Mother;
Watch over thee then will I.
And if in a far-away dream you start
I'll sing thee lullaby.
It's many – Oh, ages and ages, Mother,
We've shared, we two. Soon now:
Thou shalt be happy, grown again young,
And I as old as thou.

Walter de la Mare 1873-1956

E. Zampighi (1859-1944) *The Centre of Attraction*

Oh, yes, my dear, you have a mother,

And she, when young, was loved by another,

And in that mother's nursery

Played her mamma, like you and me.

When that mamma was tiny as you

She had a happy mother too:

On, on Yes, presto! Puff! Pee-fee! -

And Grandam Eve and the apple-tree.

O, into distance, smalling, dimming,

Think of that endless row of women,

Like beads, like posts, like lamps, they seem -

Grey-green willows, and life a stream -

Laughing and sighing and lovely; and, oh,

You to be next in that long row!

Walter de la Mare 1873-1956

L. Tuxen (1853-1927) 'The Coffee is Poured'

34

Harriet Elizabeth Beecher Stowe, (1811-1896)

'Never had any mother? What do you mean?
Where were you born?' Persisted Topsy; 'never had no
father, nor mother, nor nothin'. I was raised by a speculator.'

Uncle Tom's Cabin

When I was small my mother did my hair
While I stood in the study, obedient,
Rehearsing foreign words encoded on the spines of books,
Taking a view of the landscaped room.
Its ornamental light dulled by real morning on
Firm hills of history and letters around me;
The favoured lake of recent books, piled and reflected by
black marble;
Creeping art and green poetry growing with me up the
walls.
I chanted titles off; she plaited down my hair;
Neatly tied up I'm launched upon the world.

*Dore	Stoneware and Porcelain
Modigliani, Sacred	Imitations, Life Studies
Circles	Wallace Stevens
Dore, Modigliani	Stoneware, Porcelain
Sacred Circles	Imitations, Life Studies
Monet at	Turner Sketches
Giverny	A Writer's Journal
Duckworth	Richard
Ortega y Gasset	Jefferies
Missing	Animals in Art
Persons	Arms and Armour
Dodds, Phaidon	Playing
Frozen Tombs	Cards
Tibetan Carpets	Unease and Angels
The Word as Image	The Word as Image

Now I plait my own hair
And it's a darker tone;
Daily scales fast; no shelved music;
I read my own books, silent and private;
Gravely I watch myself's reflected flicker past my face;
Late, every morning, I upbraid myself.

Tabitha Tuckett aged 14

*These two plaits are meant to be read simultaneously by two voices.

Henry Tonks (1862-1937) *Rustic Pageantry*

Sandro Botticelli (1440-1510) *Madonna of the Eucharist*

Oh hush thee, my baby,
Thy cradle's in pawn:
No blanket to cover thee
Cold and forlorn.
The stars in the bright sky
Look down and are dumb
At the heir of the ages
Asleep in a slum.

The hooters are blowing,
No heed let him take:
When baby is hungry
'Tis best not to wake.
Thy mother is crying,
Thy dad's on the dole:
Two shillings a week is
The price of a soul.

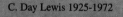

C. Day Lewis 1925-1972

Mary Cassatt (1844-1926) *Mother Combing Sara's Hair*

Lucas Cranach (1472-1553) *Head of the Virgin*

I sing of a maiden
    That is makeles;
King of all kings
    To her son she ches.

He came al so still
    There his mother was,
As dew in April
    That falleth on the grass.

He came al so still
    To his mother's bour,
As dew in April
    That falleth on the flour.

He came al so still
    There his mother lay,
As dew in April
    That falleth on the spray.

Mother and maiden
    Was never none but she;
Well may such a lady
    Goddes mother be.

Anon. 15th Century

Maurice Denis (1870-1943) *The Mellerio Family*

Like

mother,

like

daughter

16th century Proverb

Gustave Wilhelm Blom (b.1853) *Figures with a Bowl of White Chrysanthemums*

From Oscar Wilde's A *Woman of No Importance*

Lord Illingworth :   People's mothers always bore me to death.
All women become like their mothers. That is
their tragedy.

Mrs Allonby: No man does. That is his.

Ditz *Hilda Nekuda's Ironing Day*

Sir Anthony Van Dyck (1599-1641) *A Family Portrait*

The little boy lost in the lonely fen,
    Led by the wand'ring light,
Began to cry, but God ever nigh,
    Appear'd like his father in white.

He kissed the child and by the hand led
    And to his mother brought,
Who in sorrow pale, thro' the lonely dale,
    Her little boy weeping sought.

William Blake (1757-1827)

Joseph Clark (1834-1926) *The Chimney Corner*

Land of Hope and Glory, Mother of the Free,
How shall we extol thee, who are born of thee?
Wider still and wider shall thy bounds be set;
God who made thee mighty, make thee mightier yet.

Arthur Christoper Benson (1862-1925)

Haynes King (1831-1904) *The Embroidery Lesson*

Maerten van Heemsskerck (1498-1574) *Family Group*

48